SWEETHEART COASTER SET

NL COLOR

▨	05 lavender - 16 yds
▨	07 pink - 62 yds

Coaster (Work 4)

Side (62 x 7 threads) (Work 2)

SWEETHEART BOX & DOILY

SWEETHEART DOILY
NL COLOR

▨	05 lavender - 62 yds
▨	07 pink - 55 yds

Sweetheart Box Top (Work 1)
Sweetheart Doily Section (Work 4)

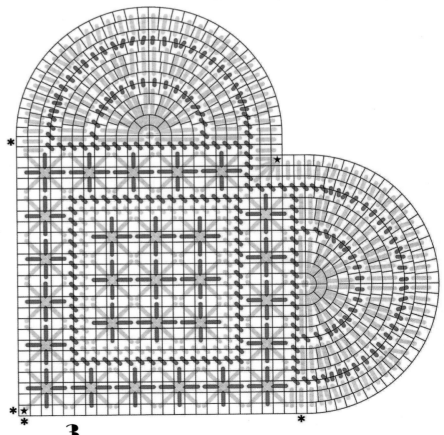

3

SWEETHEART BOX

NL COLOR

✏ 05 lavender - 36 yds

✏ 07 pink - 69 yds

Sweetheart Box Top Side (66 x 6 threads) (Work 2)

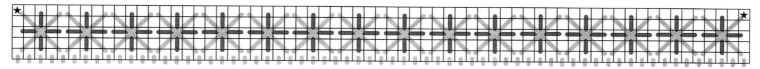

Sweetheart Box Bottom Side (63 x 17 threads) (Work 2)

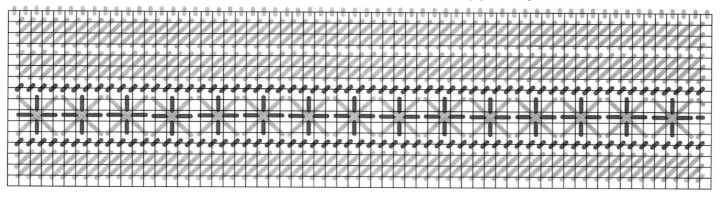

DADDY'S TREASURE PHOTO FRAME

NL COLOR

✏ 02 Christmas red - 3 yds

✏ 23 fern - 3 yds

✏ 32 royal - 3 yds

✏ 41 white - 8 yds

NL COLOR

✏ 57 yellow - 3 yds

✏ 58 bright orange - 3 yds

✏ 64 bright purple - 3 yds

✏ blue embroidery floss - 3 yds

Daddy's Treasure Front

Daddy's Treasure Back (27 x 27 threads)

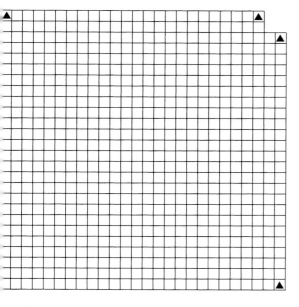

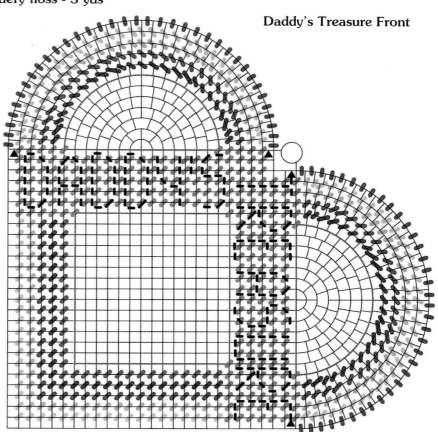

4

MOON & STARS MOBILE

NL COLOR

- 01 gold cord - 35 yds
- 02 blue cord - 57 yds

Mobile Base Front/Back (Work 2)

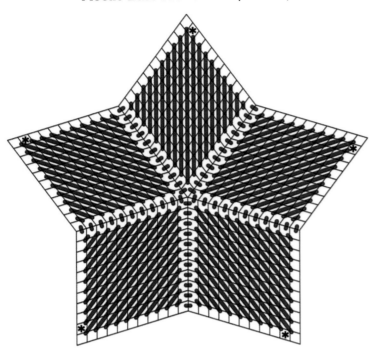

Star A Front/Back (Work 2)

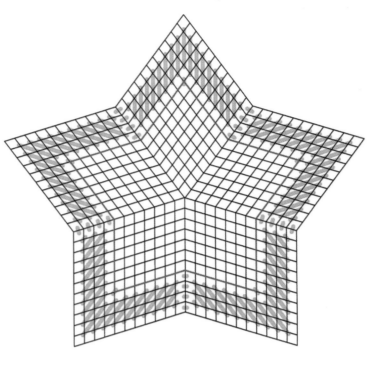

Star B Front/Back (Work 2)

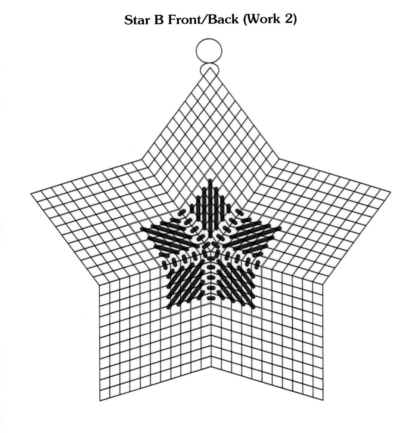

Star C Front/Back (Work 2)

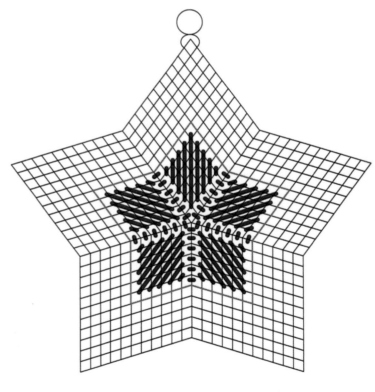

Star D Front/Back (Work 2)

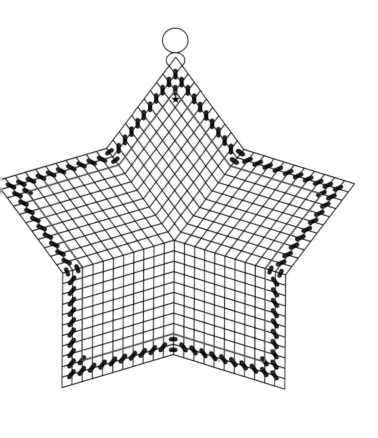

Star E Front/Back (Work 2)

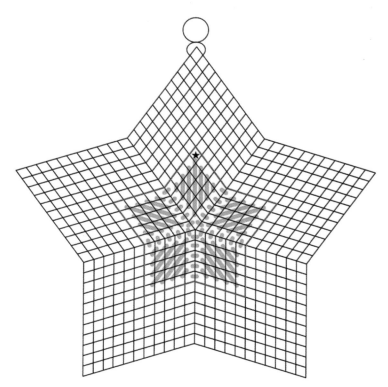

Star F Front/Back (Work 2)

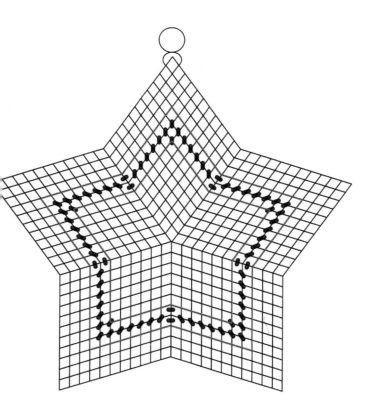

Moon Front/Back (32 x 36 threads) (Work 2)

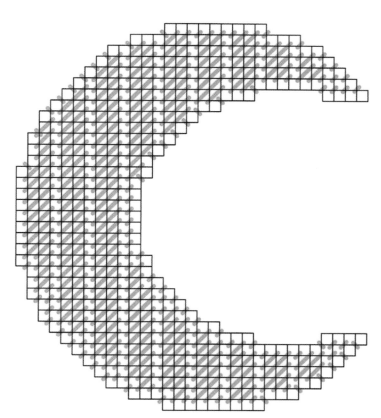

MOON & STARS COASTER SET

NL COLOR

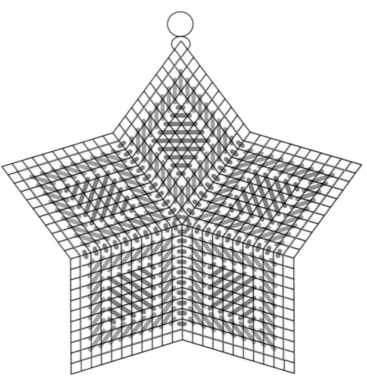 41 white - 24 yds

 08 white/silver cord - 15 yds

Silver Star (Work 2)

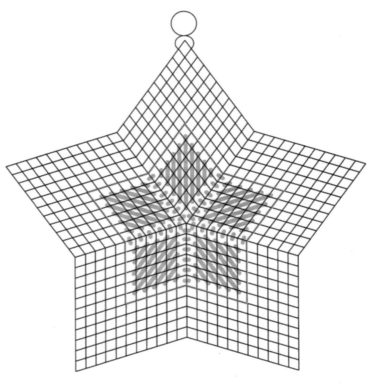

Moon (32 x 36 threads) (Work 2)

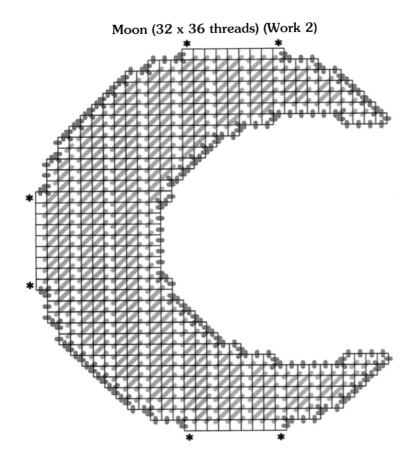

Connector (10 x 9 threads) (Work 3)

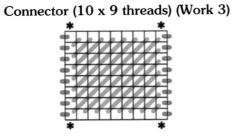

Star Coaster (Work 4)

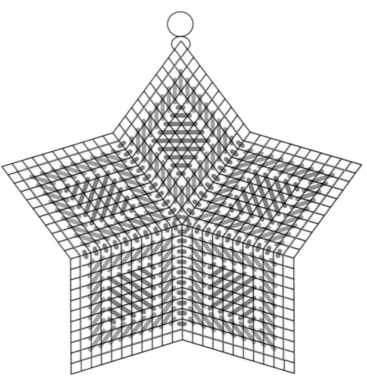

7

TAR BOXES

BLUE & SILVER
NL COLOR

☑ 32 royal - 32 yds

☐ 35 sail blue - 15 yds

☐ 08 white/silver cord - 16 yds

COUNTRY
NL COLOR

☑ 01 red - 32 yds

☐ 39 eggshell - 16 yds

☐ 48 royal dark - 15 yds

Top

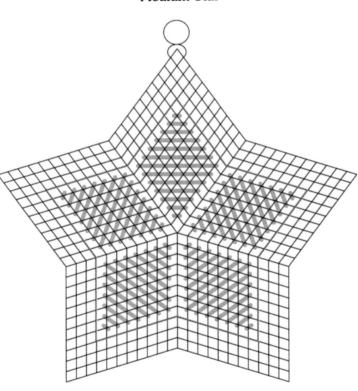

Small Star

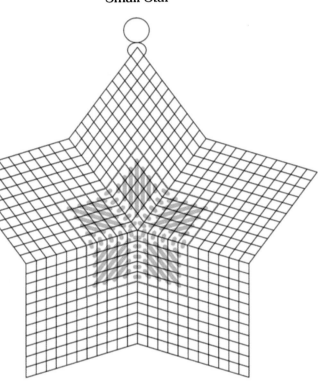

Medium Star

Bottom Side
(11 x 18 threads)
(Work 10)

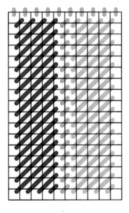

Top Side
(12 x 6 threads) (Work 10)

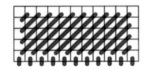

ORNAMENTS

NL COLOR

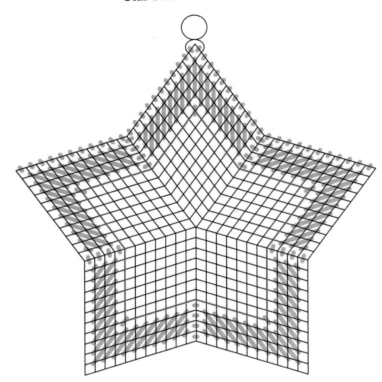

- ▨ 41 white
- ▨ 01 white/gold cord
- ▨ 26 rainbow/white cord
- ▨   iridescent white

Hexagon Photo Frame Front

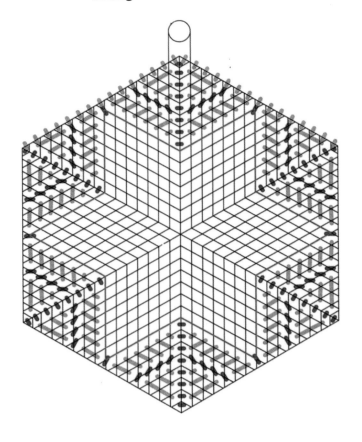

Star Photo Frame Front

Snowflake (Work 2)

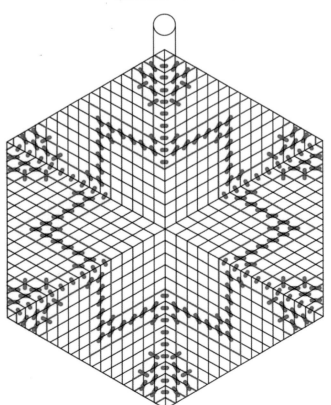

Center (Work 2)

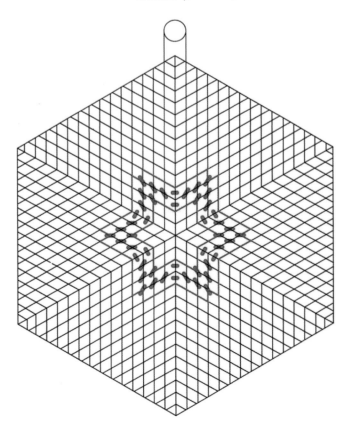

HEXAGON DOILIES

SOUTHWEST NL COLOR	COUNTRY NL COLOR
39 eggshell - 10 yds	01 red - 20 yds
51 aqua - 28 yds	39 eggshell - 10 yds
56 flesh tone - 20 yds	14 cinnamon - 28 yds

Doily Side (Work 6)

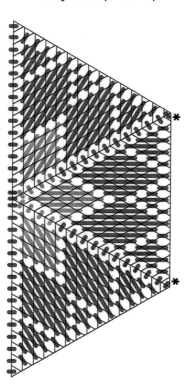

Doily Center

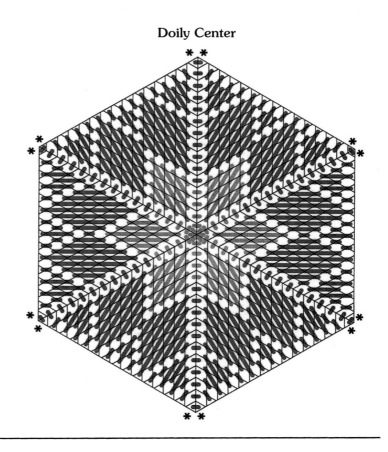

SOUTHWEST VASE

NL COLOR

- 06 rose - 22 yds
- 51 aqua - 16 yds
- 56 flesh tone - 21 yds

Vase Side (Work 8)

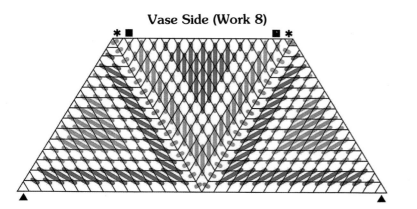

Rim (19 x 5 threads) (Work 4)

Bottom (19 x 19 threads)

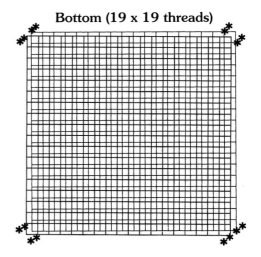

HEART POCKET

NL	COLOR		NL	COLOR
01	red - 7 yds		29	forest - 3 yds
14	cinnamon - 2 yds		39	eggshell - 12 yds
27	holly - 4 yds			

Heart Pocket Back

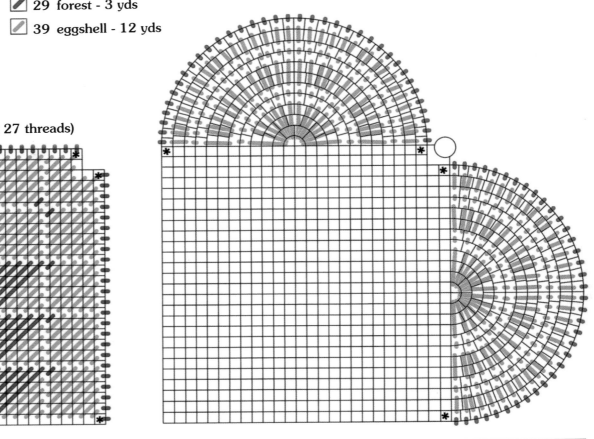

Heart Pocket Front (27 x 27 threads)

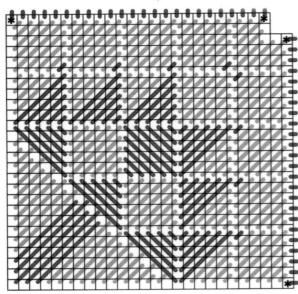

BUTTERFLY MAGNET

Wings

NL	COLOR		NL	COLOR
00	black - 8 yds		57	yellow - 6 yds
52	bittersweet - 3 yds		60	bright blue - 3 yds

Body (26 x 26 threads)

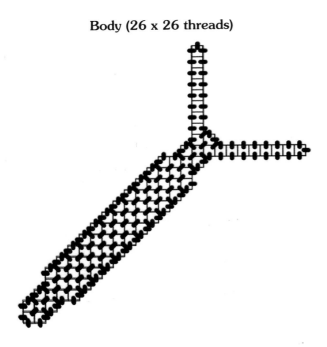

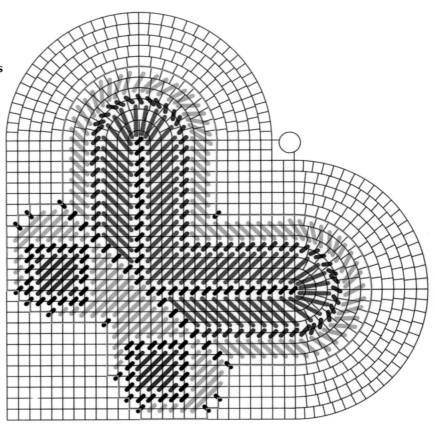

11

UPRIGHT CROSS STITCH

Fig. 11

This stitch is worked over two threads as shown in **Fig. 11**. It is sometimes worked over three or more threads. The top stitch of each cross must always be made in the same direction.

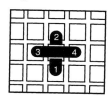

UNIQUE SHAPES
GENERAL INSTRUCTIONS

1. **Fig. 1, page 1**, shows how to count 7 mesh plastic canvas threads accurately. Follow charts to cut out 7 mesh pieces. When entire Uniek® Plastic Canvas Shape is not to be used, follow chart to cut out piece along colored cutting lines.
2. Backstitches used for detail *(Fig. 2, page 1)* are worked over completed stitches.
3. Overcast Stitches *(Fig. 7, page 1)* are used to cover the edges of pieces and to join pieces.

PROJECTS
BLUE & SILVER STAR BOX

(Color charts are on page 8.)
Size: 5½"w x 5½"h x 4¼"d
Supplies: Needloft® Plastic Canvas Yarn or worsted weight yarn (refer to color key), Needloft® #08 white/silver Metallic Cord, four Uniek® 5" star shapes, one 10½" x 13½" sheet of 7 mesh plastic canvas, #16 tapestry needle, one 18mm clear faceted bead, one 5mm silver bead cap, one clear seed bead, #28 gauge wire, and clear-drying craft glue
Instructions: Refer to charts to cut Medium Star and Small Star from 5" star shapes along pink cutting lines. Follow charts and use required stitches to work Blue & Silver Star Box pieces. Use yarn color to match stitching area to cover edges of Medium Star and Small Star with Overcast Stitches. For Bottom, cut one thread from outer edge of remaining 5" star shape. *(Note: Bottom is not worked.)* Use white/silver cord to join short unworked edges of Bottom Sides to Bottom. Use white/silver cord to join Bottom Sides along long edges. Use royal to join long unworked edges of Top Sides to Top. Use royal to join Top Sides along short edges. Refer to photo to glue Medium Star to Top. Glue Small Star to Medium Star. Center clear seed bead on a 10" length of wire. Thread both ends of wire through silver bead cap and clear faceted bead. Refer to photo to thread both ends of wire through Small Star, Medium Star, and Top. Hide ends of wire under stitches on wrong side of Top.

BUTTERFLY MAGNET

(Color charts are on page 11.)
Size: 5¼"w x 4½"h
Supplies: Needloft® Plastic Canvas Yarn (refer to color key), one Uniek® 6" heart shape, one 10½" x 13½" sheet of 7 mesh plastic canvas, #16 tapestry needle, magnetic strip, and clear-drying craft glue
Instructions: Refer to chart to cut Wings from 6" heart shape along blue cutting line. Follow charts and use required stitches to work Wings and Body. Use black Overcast Stitches to cover unworked edges. Refer to photo to glue Body to Wings. Glue magnetic strip to wrong side of stitched piece.

COUNTRY HEXAGON DOILY

(Color charts are on page 10.)
Size: 11"w x 9½"h
Supplies: Needloft® Plastic Canvas Yarn or worsted weight yarn (refer to color key), four Uniek® 5" hexagon shapes, #16 tapestry needle, cork or felt (optional), and clear-drying craft glue
Instructions: For Doily Sides, carefully cut three 5" hexagon shapes exactly in half between the doubled center threads. Follow charts and use required stitches to work Country Hexagon Doily pieces. Use cinnamon and match ✱'s to join Doily Sides to Doily Center. Use cinnamon to join Doily Sides. If backing is desired, cut cork or felt slightly smaller than stitched piece and glue to wrong side of Country Hexagon Doily.

COUNTRY STAR BOX

(Color charts are on page 8.)
Size: 5½"w x 5½"h x 3¼"d
Supplies: Needloft® Plastic Canvas Yarn or worsted weight yarn (refer to color key), four Uniek® 5" star shapes, one 10½" x 13½" sheet of 7 mesh plastic canvas, #16 tapestry needle, and clear-drying craft glue
Instructions: Refer to charts to cut Medium Star and Small Star from 5" star shapes along pink cutting lines. Follow charts and use required stitches to work Country Star Box pieces. Use yarn color to match stitching area to cover edges of Medium Star and Small Star with Overcast Stitches. For Bottom, cut one thread from outer edge of remaining 5" star shape. *(Note: Bottom is not worked.)* Use eggshell to join short unworked edges of Bottom Sides to Bottom. Use eggshell to join Bottom Sides along long edges. Use red to join long unworked edges of Top Sides to Top. Use red to join Top Sides along short edges. Refer to photo to glue Medium Star to Top. Glue Small Star to Medium Star. Refer to photo to thread a 12" length of red yarn through Top, Medium Star, and Small Star. Tie yarn in a bow and trim ends.

DADDY'S TREASURE PHOTO FRAME

(Color chart is on page 4.)
Size: 6⅝"w x 6"h
(Note: Opening is 2¾"w x 2¾"h.)
Supplies: Needloft® Plastic Canvas Yarn or worsted weight yarn (refer to color key), blue embroidery floss, one Uniek® 6" heart shape, one 10½" x 13½" sheet of 7 mesh plastic canvas, #16 tapestry needle, 12" length of ⅜"w blue satin ribbon, and clear-drying craft glue
Instructions: Refer to chart to cut Front from a 6" heart shape along blue cutting lines. Use six strands of embroidery floss for Backstitch. Follow chart and use required stitches to work Front. Refer to photo for colors of Overcast Stitches to cover inner edges of Front. Use Christmas red and match ▲'s to join Front to Back along unworked edges of Front. Tie ribbon in a bow and trim ends. Refer to photo to glue bow to Daddy's Treasure Photo Frame.

HEART POCKET

(Color charts are on page 11.)
Size: 6⅝"w x 6"h
Supplies: Needloft® Plastic Canvas Yarn or worsted weight yarn (refer to color key), one Uniek® 6" heart shape, one 10½" x 13½" sheet of 7 mesh plastic canvas, #16 tapestry needle, 12" length of ⅜"w red satin ribbon, and clear-drying craft glue
Instructions: Follow charts and use required stitches to work Heart Pocket pieces. Match ✱'s to place Front on Back. Use red to join Front to Back along unworked edges. Tie ribbon in a bow and trim ends. Refer to photo to glue bow to Heart Pocket.

HEXAGON PHOTO FRAME ORNAMENT

(Color chart is on page 9.)
Size: 5"w x 6"h
(Note: Opening is 4"w x 3½"h.)
Supplies: Needloft® #26 rainbow/white Frizzette Metallic Cord, two Uniek® 5" hexagon shapes, and #16 tapestry needle
Instructions: Refer to chart to cut Hexagon Photo Frame Front from a 5" hexagon shape along blue cutting line. Follow chart and use required stitches to work Front. Use rainbow/white cord Overcast Stitches to cover inner edges of Front. For Back, place remaining 5" hexagon shape on the wrong side of Front, aligning hangers and edges. *(Note: Back is not worked.)* Refer to photo and use rainbow/white cord to join Front to Back along unworked edges of Front. Refer to photo to tie a 12" length of rainbow/white cord in a bow around hangers and trim ends.

MOON & STARS COASTER SET

(Color charts are on page 7.)
Holder Size: 5½"w x 5½"h x 1¾"d
Coaster Size: 5"w x 5"h each
Supplies: Needloft® #41 white Plastic Canvas Yarn or white worsted weight yarn, Needloft® white/silver Metallic Cord, six Uniek® 5" star shapes, one 10½" x 13½" sheet of 7 mesh plastic canvas, #16 tapestry needle, white felt, and clear-drying craft glue
Instructions: Refer to charts to cut Star Coasters and Silver Stars from 5" star shapes along pink cutting lines. Follow charts and use required stitches to work Star Coasters and Coaster Holder pieces. Use white Overcast Stitches to cover edges of Star Coasters. For backing, cut felt slightly smaller than Star Coaster and glue to wrong side of stitched piece. Use white/silver cord Overcast Stitches to cover edges of Silver Stars. Refer to photo, use white/silver cord, and match ✱'s to join Connectors to Moons. Refer to photo to glue Silver Stars to Moons.

MOON & STARS MOBILE

(Color charts are on pages 5 and 6.)
Approx Size: 10"w x 26½"h x 10"d
Supplies: Needloft® Metallic Cord (refer to color key), fourteen Uniek® 5" star shapes, one 10½" x 13½" sheet of 7 mesh plastic canvas, #16 tapestry needle, 5mm round gold beads, gold rochaille beads, ⅝"w gold star sequins, nylon line, and #26 tapestry needle (for working with nylon line)
Instructions: Refer to charts to cut Stars from 5" star shapes along pink cutting lines. Follow charts and use required stitches to work Mobile pieces. Use color to match stitching area to join Fronts to Backs. Cut five 24" lengths of blue cord. Tie a knot at one end of each length. Thread loose end of one length through each point of Mobile Base at ✱'s, leaving knots on underside of Base. Tie all lengths together in a knot 8" above Mobile Base. Tie all lengths together in a second knot 2½" above first knot. Refer to photo and use nylon line to tack Star E inside Star D at ★'s. Cut six 14" lengths of nylon line. Tack one end of each length to Moon and Stars A, B, C, D, and F. Tie first rochaille beads to nylon lines 1" from stitched pieces. Thread desired number of round beads and sequins onto nylon lines and tie second rochaille beads above round beads and sequins. Repeat bead and sequin pattern until nylon lines have been filled to lengths indicated in Diagram. Refer to Diagram to tie loose end of nylon line on Moon to the center of Mobile Base. Refer to Diagram to tie loose ends of nylon lines on Stars A, B, C, D, and F to the points of Mobile Base. Trim ends of nylon lines.

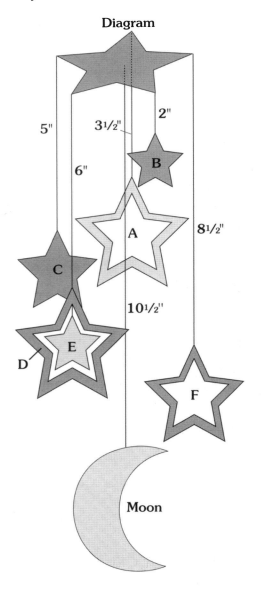

Diagram

13